W9-BJN-024

Funniest Bone Animal Jokes

HUMOROUS
Small Critter
JOKES
to Tickle Your
FUNNY BONE

Susan K. Mitchell

Enslow Elementary
an imprint of
Enslow Publishers, Inc.
40 Industrial Road
Box 398
Berkeley Heights, NJ 07922
USA

http://www.enslow.com

For Emily the Limerick Queen. And to Jude, Ava, Jack, and Zayne—thanks for the laughs!

Enslow Elementary, an imprint of Enslow Publishers, Inc.

Enslow Elementary® is a registered trademark of Enslow Publishers, Inc.

Library of Congress Cataloging-in-Publication Data
Mitchell, Susan K.
Humorous small critter jokes to tickle your funny bone / by Susan K. Mitchell.
pages cm. — (Funniest bone animal jokes)
Includes index.
Summary: "Read jokes, limericks, tongue twisters, and knock-knock jokes about mice and other small creatures. Also find out fun facts about these animals"—Provided by publisher.
ISBN 978-0-7660-6032-6
1. Animals—Juvenile humor. I. Title.
PN6231.A5M58 2014
818'.602080362—dc23
$\qquad$ 2013008790

Future editions:
Paperback ISBN: 978-0-7660-6033-3 $\qquad$ EPUB ISBN: 978-0-7660-6034-0
Single-User PDF ISBN: 978-0-7660-6035-7 $\quad$ Multi-User PDF ISBN: 978-0-7660-6036-4

Printed in the United States of America
072014 HF Group, North Manchester, IN
10 9 8 7 6 5 4 3 2 1

To Our Readers: We have done our best to make sure all Internet addresses in this book were active and appropriate when we went to press. However, the author and the publisher have no control over and assume no liability for the material available on those Internet sites or on other Web sites they may link to. Any comments or suggestions can be sent by e-mail to comments@enslow.com or to the address on the back cover.

Every effort has been made to locate all copyright holders of material used in this book. If any errors or omissions have occurred, corrections will be made in future editions of this book.

Illustration Credits: Clipart.com: 4 (bottom), 5 (top and middle right), 6 (top), 7 (top), 8 (bottom), 9 (both at bottom), 10 (all), 13 (all), 15 (bottom), 17 (bottom), 18 (top), 19 (top), 20 (top), 21 (all), 22 (top), 23 (all), 24 (all), 25 (all), 26 (middle), 27 (middle), 28 (top), 29, 30 (top),31 (bottom), 32 (middle, bottom), 33 (all), 34 (both at top), 36 (all), 38 (bottom), 39 (middle); Shutterstock.com: 4 (top, middle), 5 (bottom right), 7 (bottom), 8 (top), 9 (top), 11 (top, middle), 14 (bottom), 15 (top), 16, 17 (both in middle), 19 (bottom) 20 (middle), 22 (middle), 26 (top, bottom), 27 (bottom), 28 (bottom), 30 (middle, bottom), 31 (middle), 32 (top), 34 (bottom), 35 (all), 37, 38 (top), 39 (top, bottom), 40 (top, middle), 41 (bottom), 42 (bottom), 43 (top), 45; © 2013 Thinkstock: (Alexei Nastoiascii/iStock) 31 (top); (Alexey Bannykh/Hemera) 3 (all), 14 (top); (Alexeyzet/iStock) 43 (bottom right); (Bob Ash/iStock) 5 (bottom left); (Dynamic Graphics/liquidlibrary/© Getty Images) 12 (bottom), 41 (middle), 43 (bottom left); (Frazer Worth/iStock/© Smokeyjo) 18 (bottom); (Igor Zakowski/Hemera) 6 (middle); (Nathan Shelton/iStock) 6 (bottom); (Oleksiy Tsuper/iStock) 42 (top); (Pablo Daniel Antuña Maquieira/iStock) 1, 5 (middle left); (Savvas Lampoudis/iStock) 40 (bottom); (Verzh/iStock) 12 (top), 27 (top).

Cover Illustrations: Matthew Cole/Shutterstock.com (front); © Igor Zakowski/Hemera/© 2013 Thinkstock (back).

Contents

1 Marvelous Mice 4

2 Really Funny Rats 8

3 Hilarious Hamsters 12

4 Giggly Guinea Pigs 16

5 Silly Shrews 20

6 Mischievous Moles 24

7 Nifty Naked Mole Rats 28

8 Goofy Gophers 32

9 Chuckling Chipmunks
   and Woodchucks 36

10 Squirrely Squirrels 40

Make a Limerick Book 44

Words to Know 46

Read More 47

Index 48

Marvelous Mice

Did you hear the joke about the mice?

Yeah, but it was really cheesy!

Nine nice mice nested neatly near the ice.

What is a mouse's favorite game?

Hide & squeak.

What is a mouse's second favorite game?

Parcheesy.

Did you hear about the mouse who won the lottery?

Yeah, he was on a winning squeak!

DID YOU KNOW?

A female mouse is called a doe, and a male is called a buck. Baby mice are sometimes referred to as pinkies. A group of mice is called a mischief.

What type of mouse plays football?

A field mouse!

Knock, knock.

Who's there?

Mice.

Mice who?

Mice to see you! Come on in!

What did the mouse eat for breakfast?

Mice Krispies.

Many moose and mice made marvelous music in the moonlight.

DID YOU KNOW?

The world's largest recorded plague of mice happened in 1993. Millions of mice invaded farmland in Australia. They destroyed crops and livestock.

Why did the mouse take a shower?

To get squeaky clean!

Knock, knock.

Who's there?

Sarah.

Sarah who?

Sarah mouse in here? I hear squeaking.

There once were some mice in Spain,
Who went out in the pouring rain.
They fashioned a boat
From an old overcoat
And sailed down the street past the drain.

Why do mice like their pictures taken?

Because they get to say, "Cheese!"

Mabel Mouse murmured for Mother Mouse to make macaroons.

What happens if a mouse doesn't shave?

He grows a mouse-stache!

Limerick

There once was a mouse named Sue,
All day there was cheese she would chew.
She liked cheddar and Swiss,
These flavors were bliss,
But her favorite by far was Bleu.

Really Funny Rats

Knock, knock.

Who's there?

Wanda.

Wanda who?

Wanda where the cheese went? Let's ask the rats.

What is a rat's favorite dinner?

Ratatouille.

Why did the rat get great grades in science?

He was a lab rat!

FUN FACT

Rats have been to space! France launched the first rat, named Hector, into space in 1961.

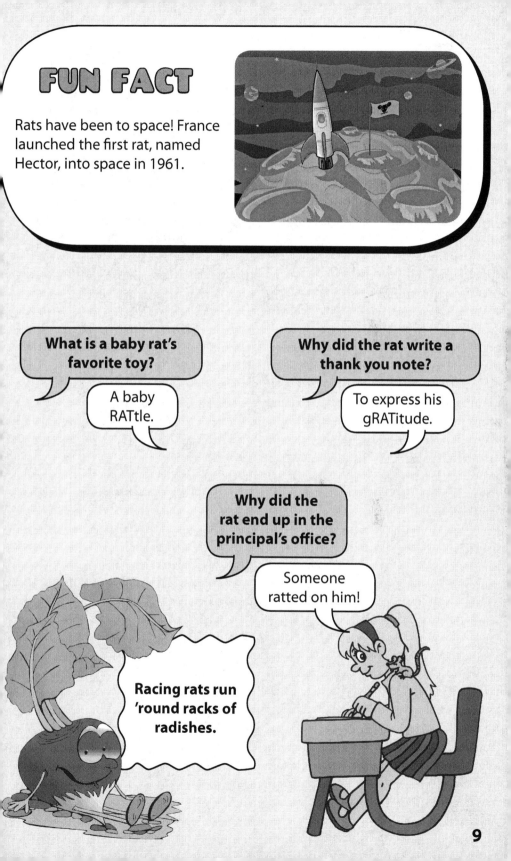

What is a baby rat's favorite toy?

A baby RATtle.

Why did the rat write a thank you note?

To express his gRATitude.

Why did the rat end up in the principal's office?

Someone ratted on him!

Racing rats run 'round racks of radishes.

Limerick

There once was a rat in the cellar,
A place that he thought was quite stellar.
It was dark and inviting,
With limited lighting—
Just right for that little cave dweller.

What kinds of rats have buried treasure?

Arrrrgh ... pi-rats!

What does a rat say when he thinks something is cool?

RAT-ical!

Knock, knock.

Who's there?

Rats.

Rats who?

Rats very nice of you to knock before you enter.

Seven rats set sail on seven ships at sea.

Limerick

A rat who was taking a trip
Decided to travel by ship.
When it started to lean,
He grew sickly and green—
He wished this one ride he could skip.

3 Hilarious Hamsters

What is a hamster's favorite book?

Green Eggs and Hamsters!

Why did the hamster run on his wheel?

Because he didn't want to cross the street!

Where do hamsters like to go on vacation?

Hamsterdam!

DID YOU KNOW?

Hamsters are thought to be color blind. In fact, they have very poor eyesight overall. Most hamsters can see only a few inches in front of them.

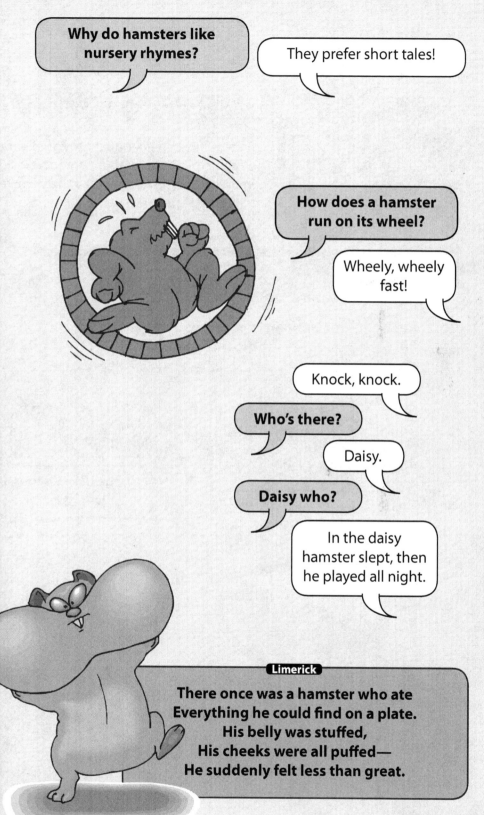

Why do hamsters like nursery rhymes?

They prefer short tales!

How does a hamster run on its wheel?

Wheely, wheely fast!

Knock, knock.

Who's there?

Daisy.

Daisy who?

In the daisy hamster slept, then he played all night.

Limerick

There once was a hamster who ate
Everything he could find on a plate.
His belly was stuffed,
His cheeks were all puffed—
He suddenly felt less than great.

13

DID YOU KNOW?

Hamsters have cheek pouches that expand. They can store large amounts of food inside them. When full, this can make the hamster head twice its normal size.

Hannah Hamster had heavenly hashbrowns and ham.

What is a hamster's favorite game show?

Wheel of Fortune.

Where do hamsters put their laundry?

In the dirty clothes hampster.

Limerick

A hamster awake through the night
Will race on his wheel with delight.
For hours he'll run,
And think, "Oh what fun!"
But fall asleep in the daylight.

Knock, knock.

Who's there?

Phillip.

Phillip who?

That hamster sure did Phillip his cheek pouches!

Willie's hamster wheel wiggled and wobbled wickedly.

Knock, knock.

Who's there?

Cedar.

Cedar who?

Cedar hamster over there running on his wheel?

What is a hamster's favorite bike trick?

Popping a wheelie!

15

4 Giggly Guinea Pigs

Why did the mother guinea pig make her son clean his room?

Because it was a guinea pigsty!

Knock, knock.

Who's there?

Gladys.

Gladys who?

Gladys guinea pig doesn't keep me up all night.

What do you call a selfish guinea pig?

A gimme pig!

What do you call an inexpensive guinea pig?

A penny pig!

DID YOU KNOW?

The largest rodent in the world is a cousin to the guinea pig. It is called a capybara and lives in South America. A capybara can grow to be more than four feet long and more than a foot tall. It can weigh more than 100 pounds. That is equal to more than 33 adult guinea pigs!

What would you call a guinea pig that laid an egg?

A henny pig!

Why did the guinea pig carry an oil can?

Because he was always squeaking!

What happened to the guinea pig after he went on a diet?

He became a skinny pig!

Guinea pigs who hail from Peru
Do nothing all day long but chew.
They nibble on sticks
'Till they look like toothpicks,
And once the wood's gone they are through.

Knock, knock.

Who's there?

Ida.

Ida who?

Ida wondered what that sound was. It's a guinea pig squealing!

Guinea pigs paint purple pencils in Pennsylvania.

Gretchen the grumpy guinea pig grumbled, griped, and groaned.

Limerick

There once was a great guinea pig
Who loved to dance a fine jig.
He danced all the day,
And at night he would play.
His life was as sweet as a fig.

FUN FACT

A guinea pig is also called a cavy. Males are called boars. Females are called sows. Even though these names are also used for pigs, guinea pigs and pigs are absolutely not related.

What does a bald guinea pig wear on his head?

A guinea wig.

What did the guinea pig use to write a letter?

A guinea pig-pen.

Many skinny guinea pigs ate any figs they could find.

What do you call a guinea pig trying to stay warm?

A guinea pig-in-a-blanket.

5 Silly Shrews

What is a shrew's favorite kind of test question?

Shrew or false!

Limerick

There once was a hungry old shrew
Who decided to cook barbecue.
When he started the fire,
The meat then turned drier—
A mess that he couldn't undo.

What did the shrew say when his brother sneezed?

"Bless shrew!"

FUN FACT

A few types of shrews are poisonous. They have a toxin in their saliva. It is not dangerous to humans, but a bite can be very painful.

What do you get when you cross a shrew and some fungus?

A mushrew-m!

What is a shrew's favorite treat?

Shrewing gum!

DID YOU KNOW?

The hero shrew, from Africa, is one amazingly strong small mammal! This tiny animal has one of the strongest spines in the world. It could carry the weight of a 160-pound human without being crushed! Most animals have five bones in their lower back. The hero shrew has eleven.

What do you get when you cross a shrew and a magician?

A voodoo shrew.

Limerick

There once was a seafaring shrew
Who wanted to sail a canoe.
Little'd he know
That he couldn't row,
When he sank, though, it gave him a clue.

Surely, Sherry Shrew should share her shawl.

What do you call a shrew who can escape a trap?

Shrew-dini!

What is a baby shrew's favorite game to play?

Peek-a-shrew.

Knock, knock.

Who's there?

Cy.

Cy who?

Cy never saw an animal as fierce as a shrew.

Knock, knock.

Who's there?

Minnie.

Minnie who?

A shrew can eat Minnie, Minnie worms.

Who knew the shrew's shoe was so full of glue?

Knock, knock.

Who's there?

Shrew.

Shrew who?

Shrew should know, shrew answered the door.

What does a shrew write after he gets a gift?

A thank-shrew note!

Seven shrieking shrews shaved shaggy sheep.

6 Mischievous Moles

What do you call a mole that lives in a churchyard?

A holy moley!

What do you get when you cross a mole with an avocado?

A guaca-moley!

A whole bowl of moles rolled past a pole in the knoll.

Why was the star-nosed mole so popular?

She was a mole lot of fun!

Knock, knock.

Who's there?

Betty.

Betty who?

Did you see that mole digging? Betty wishes he had a shovel.

How did the blind mole cross the street?

With a seeing-eye chicken!

DID YOU KNOW?

Moles dig for food constantly. A mole can die of starvation if it does not eat every few hours.

Maybe mild-mannered moles make many mistakes.

Woe be to the wandering, wayward worm who wiggles when a mole is nearby.

Knock, knock.

Who's there?

Nita.

Nita who?

No Nita make a mountain out of a molehill.

Limerick

There once was an old, blind mole
Who lived underground in a hole.
He dug tunnels all day,
Never stopping to play,
It was true he's a lonely old soul.

Knock, knock.

Who's there?

Bill Eve.

Bill Eve who?

I Bill Eve that poor mole could use some eyeglasses.

Limerick

A mole who was lacking in sight
Dug tunnels with all of his might.
One day, somehow,
He got hit by a plow,
Then 'cross the field he took flight.

What is a mole's favorite music?

Rock 'n mole!

Why didn't the mole eat his sandwich?

It was mole-dy.

What is a mole's favorite play?

Mole-meo & Juliet.

How did the mole solve the math problem?

He used mole-tiplication.

27

Nifty Naked Mole Rats

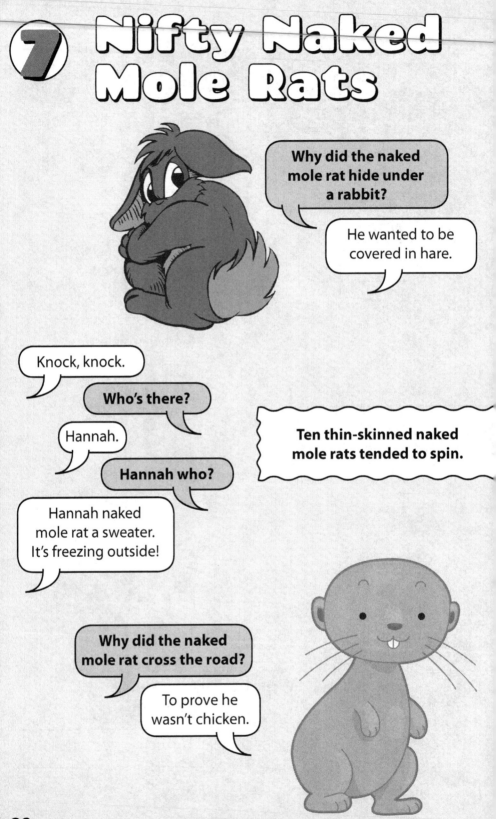

Why did the naked mole rat hide under a rabbit?

He wanted to be covered in hare.

Knock, knock.

Who's there?

Hannah.

Hannah who?

Hannah naked mole rat a sweater. It's freezing outside!

Ten thin-skinned naked mole rats tended to spin.

Why did the naked mole rat cross the road?

To prove he wasn't chicken.

What does a naked mole rat rub on after a bath?

Wrinkle cream.

Why did everyone think the naked mole rat was so brave?

He was furless.

Limerick

There once was a mole rat from France
Who refused to wear any pants.
Some thought it was rude
When he showed up nude,
So they kicked him right out of the dance.

Why couldn't the naked mole rat take a joke?

Because he was thin skinned.

Which side of a naked mole rat has the most wrinkly, pink skin?

The outside.

DID YOU KNOW?

Naked mole rats are neither moles nor rats. They are more closely related to porcupines and guinea pigs.

29

Knock, knock.

Who's there?

Donna.

Donna who?

I Donna know why the naked mole rat isn't wearing fur!

What do you call a naked mole rat that can pick up an elephant?

Anything he wants you to call him!

FUN FACT

Naked mole rats live in colonies of 200 to 300 members. Like bees, they have a queen, workers, and soldiers.

Naughty naked mole rats nibbled and gnawed at nighttime.

DID YOU KNOW?

Like most rodents, gophers' teeth never stop growing. They can grow up to 14 inches each year. Gophers have to chew to keep them short.

What does the gopher think of disco music?

He digs it, man.

What is a gopher's favorite carnival ride?

The tunnel of love.

TUNNEL OF ♥ LOVE ♥

FUN FACT

Many animals move into empty gopher burrows. Snakes, armadillos, and lizards are just a few animals that like to live in the abandoned tunnels.

Giggling gophers guzzled gobs of green goop.

Daring, dashing gophers dug dazzlingly deep dens.

Knock, knock.

Who's there?

Candy.

Candy who?

Candy gopher dig a long tunnel? He sure can!

Limerick

There once was a young gopher lad,
When he golfed, he always wore plaid.
He'd hit the ball far,
For birdie or par,
And his hole-in-one wasn't half bad.

SNAP!

9 Chuckling Chipmunks & Woodchucks

What do you call a chipmunk eating Mexican food?

A chipmunk and salsa.

Why did the chipmunk get in trouble with his mother?

He was being cheeky.

Why wouldn't the chipmunk spend his money?

He was a cheap-munk.

Chester Chipmunk's cheeks were chock-full of chilled chestnuts.

DID YOU KNOW?

There are 25 different types of chipmunks. All but one of them are found in North America.

What do you get when you cross a chipmunk and a skunk?

A chipstunk.

Knock, knock.

Who's there?

Carrie.

Carrie who?

That chipmunk can Carrie nuts in his cheeks.

What do you call a chipmunk in the Navy?

A ship-munk.

Cheery, chubby chipmunks chewed chewy chocolate cherries.

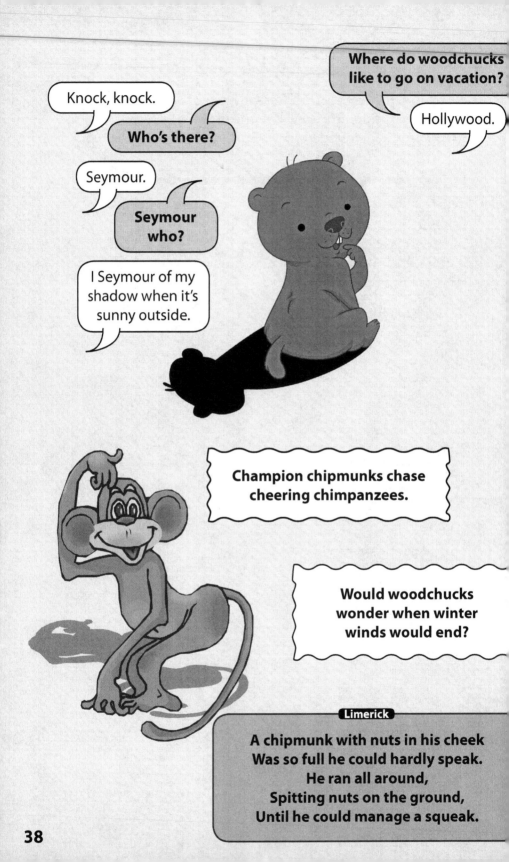

Why didn't the woodchuck trust his own shadow?

Because it was kind of shady.

What does a woodchuck use to play hockey?

A woodchuck puck.

Limerick

On February second each year,
Woodchucks emerge to a cheer.
On a tree stump they perch,
For their shadow they search.
If they find it, then spring is not near.

Knock, knock.

Who's there?

Cash.

Cash who?

"No thanks," said the squirrel. "I'd rather have acorns."

Why did the squirrel board an airplane?

Because she was a flying squirrel.

Knock, knock.

Who's there?

Scott.

Scott who?

Scott to be hard for a squirrel to find all his hidden nuts.

Limerick

There once was a squirrel named Cy,
Who decided he wanted to fly.
He soared and he glided,
His talent was prided,
Each time he took to the sky.

FUN FACT

Flying squirrels do not really fly. They glide through the air using special flaps of skin. Some have been known to glide an amazing distance of almost 300 feet.

What do you call a squirrel with four corners?

A squarel.

Six squeaky squirrels squeezed some squishy squash.

What is a squirrel's favorite musical instrument?

An acornion.

Did you hear the joke about the squirrel?

Yeah, it was acorn-y one!

Limerick

There once was an acrobat squirrel,
All day through the forest she'd twirl.
She flew through the trees,
Like they were trapeze.
In the breeze, her bushy tail'd whirl.

Make a Limerick Book

Limericks are a fun form of poetry. They were made popular by a writer named Edward Lear. In the 1840s, he wrote *A Book of Nonsense*, which was full of silly limericks. You can create your own book of these short, hilarious poems.

What you will need:

- plain white paper—at least two pieces, cut in half crosswise

- one large loose rubber band or a stapler with staples

- colored pencils, markers, or crayons

Rules for writing a limerick:

– The first, second, and fifth lines rhyme with each other. These lines have eight to ten syllables.

– The third and fourth lines rhyme. These lines have four to five syllables.

– The first line in a limerick usually ends with a name or place.

– The last line is usually funny or unexpected.

Getting started:

1. Pick a name or place to use in the first line.

2. Use a rhyming dictionary to find words that will go with that first line. These can be used at the end of lines two and five.

3. Write lines one, two, and five first. Then go back and write lines three and four. It can be easier that way.

Example:

There once was a mouse named Louise
Who alas was allergic to cheese.
She couldn't go near,
The poor little dear—
If she got near the cheese, she would sneeze.

How to create the book:

. Fold each piece of paper in half crosswise.

2. Place one of the pieces of folded paper in the middle of the other. These will be the pages of your book. You can use more paper. Just continue folding paper and putting the pages together.

3. Slide the rubber band around the paper until it reaches the fold of the paper in the middle of the book. This will hold the pages together. If you prefer, staple the pages along the fold.

4. Write a limerick on each page. Use colored pencils, crayons, or markers to illustrate. Don't forget your title page, with your name as the author!

Words to Know

cheeky—Sassy.

gopher—A burrowing rodent with a thick body, short legs, and cheek pouches found in North America.

groundhog—Another name for a woodchuck, which is a burrowing rodent with a thick body and thick fur.

joke—Something that is said to make people laugh.

limerick—A funny five-line poem in which the first, second, and fifth lines rhyme, and the shorter third and fourth lines rhyme.

mole—A small underground mammal with velvety fur and small eyes.

naked mole rat—A small, hairless African rodent with extremely large front teeth.

Punxsutawney—A town in Pennsylvania that hosts a huge Groundhog Day celebration each year.

rodent—Any of a group of mammals known for their large, constantly growing front teeth.

shrew—A small, mouse-like mammal with a long, pointed nose; shrews eat only insects.

tongue twister—A series of fun words that can be hard to say out loud.

Read More

Books

Connolly, Sean. *The Animal Antics Joke Book*. New York: Windmill Books, 2011.

Dahl, Michael. *The Funny Farm: Jokes About Dogs, Cats, Ducks, Snakes, Bears, and Other Animals*. North Mankato, Minn.: Picture Window Books, 2010.

Winter, Judy A. *Jokes About Animals*. North Mankato, Minn.: Capstone Press, 2010.

Internet Addresses

Aha! Jokes: Kids Jokes: Animal Jokes
http://www.ahajokes.com/animal_jokes_for_kids.html

Limerick Factory
http://www.learner.org/teacherslab/math/patterns/limerick/limerick_acttxt.html

Ducksters: Jokes: Big list of kids animal jokes
http://www.ducksters.com/jokesforkids/animals.php

Index

A

Africa, 21
armadillos, 35
Australia, 6

B

bees, 30
boars (male guinea pigs), 19
bucks (male mice), 5
burrows, 35

C

capybaras, 17
cavies, 19
cheek pouches, 14
chipmunks, 36–38
colonies, 30
color blindness, 12

D

does (female mice), 5

E

eyesight, 12

F

flying squirrels, 42, 43
France, 9

G

gophers, 32–35
groundhogs, 39
guinea pigs, 16–19, 29

H

hamsters, 12–15
Hector (space rat), 9
hero shrews, 21

L

lizards, 35

M

mice, 4–7
mischief (group of mice), 5
moles, 24–27, 29

N

naked mole rats, 28–31
North America, 37

P

pigs, 19
pinkies (baby mice), 5
plagues, 6
porcupines, 29
Punxsutawney Phil, 39

Q

queen (naked mole rat), 30

R

rats, 8–11, 29
rodents, 17, 33

S

shrews, 20–23
snakes, 35
soldiers (naked mole rats), 30
South America, 17
sows (female guinea pigs), 19
space, 9
squirrels, 40–43
star-nosed moles, 24
starvation, 25

T

teeth, 33
toxins, 20

W

woodchucks, 38, 39
workers (naked mole rats), 30